Henry Larsen

John Bassett

Fitzhenry & Whiteside Limited

Contents

The Canadians A continuing series

General Editor: Robert Read
Consulting Editor: Roderick Stewart
Designer: Jack Steiner
Editors: Laura Damania, Rosalind Sharpe

Bassett, John M., 1920-
Henry Larsen

(The Canadians)

Bibliography: p. 64
ISBN 0-88902-230-5

1. Larsen, Henry A., 1899-1964. 2. Canada. Royal Canadian Mounted Police — Biography. 3. Arctic regions — Canadian exploration. I. Series.

FC3216.3.L37B38   363.2'092'4   C79-094761-7
HV7911.L37B38

The Author

John M. Bassett was for many years associated with the Lincoln County Board of Education, and has written many historical studies for young readers.

© *1980, Fitzhenry & Whiteside Limited*
150 Lesmill Road
Don Mills, Ontario M3B 2T5

Printed and bound in Canada

Opening up the Arctic Chapter 1

Winter was ready to settle over Vancouver Harbour and the islands along the Pacific coast. Before shipping ended for the season, however, a small R.C.M.P. schooner, the *St. Roch*, slipped into harbour. It was not a handsome craft, and even in dock it seemed to pitch and toss more than the other ships. But the fact that it was an exceptional vessel was attested by the news that it had twice completed the gruelling voyage along the northern edge of the North American continent, through the treacherous Northwest Passage.

Only one other ship had ever made that trip. From 1903 to 1906, Roald Amundsen took the *Gjoa* through the shallow, coastal waters of the Arctic Ocean and succeeded in crossing from the Atlantic to the Pacific. From 1940-42, Sergeant Henry Larsen steered the *St. Roch* along almost the same route, but in the opposite direction, becoming the second man and first Canadian to sail the Northwest Passage and the first to do so from west to east. In 1944, Larsen brought the *St. Roch* from Halifax to Vancouver along a more northerly route which had never before been navigated.

For four centuries before Larsen's successful conquest of the Arctic, explorers had been trying to find a way from Europe to the Far East by way of the Northwest Passage. In spite of their skill, courage and determination, successive explorers were defeated by the uncharted, icy seas and the killing cold.

Although the obstacles presented by nature were terrible, the early explorers were confident that the rewards for finding a route to the "Indies" would more than make up for the hardships of the voyage. In the fifteenth century, stories of the fabulous wealth of China, or "Cathay," were current in Europe, but the voyage around Africa was long and dangerous. Many people believed that a short, direct route to the East lay through the Northwest Passage and that to find it they needed only to sail west and north.

The search was on. John Cabot is generally credited as the first explorer to seek the northern route. In 1497 he sailed from England and after 52 days reached land, convinced that he had arrived in Asia. In fact, Cabot had probably reached the shores of Newfoundland, and he returned without the spices and silks of China. He did not lose hope, however, and the next year set sail once more with a fleet of five ships. All five were lost at sea. Cabot and his men were the first of many to perish in the search for the Northwest Passage.

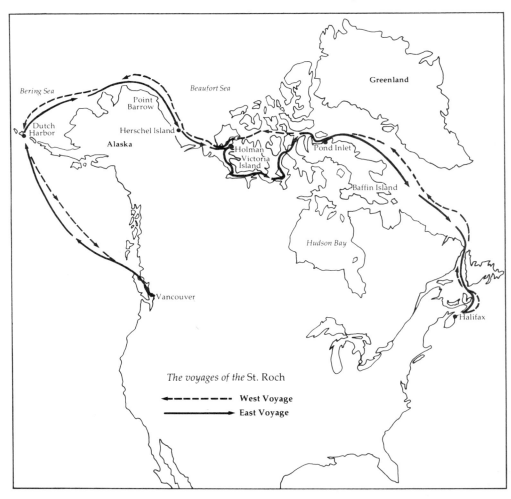

The voyages of the St. Roch

← – – – – – ·   **West Voyage**
──────→   **East Voyage**

The next serious attempt to discover the northern route was made in 1576, almost eighty years after Cabot's death. The leader of the expedition, Martin Frobisher, had a fleet of three vessels, the *Gabriel* and *Michael* both of twenty-three tons, and a pinnace of only nine tons. It took tremendous courage to sail such tiny ships into dangerous and unknown waters. Sadly, the expedition met with constant trouble. First came the sinking of the pinnace and the loss of the entire crew. Then five men sent ashore for fresh water disappeared completely. Some of the Inuit the explorers encountered were hostile and the frustrated sailors threatened mutiny. Frobisher was forced to return to England. He made two more trips without finding the passage, but returned to England both times with ships laden with ore. Frobisher believed that he had a fortune in gold, but it turned out to be worthless rock.

Sir Martin Frobisher

Frobisher found neither wealth nor a passage to China, but he made a valuable contribution to the Arctic adventure. He charted the coast as far as the bay on Baffin Island that now bears his name, and showed that brave and resourceful explorers could penetrate the Arctic and return alive.

John Davis (right) plans his voyage of discovery with three famous Elizabethan courtiers, Dr. Dee, Adrian Gilbert and Sir Francis Walsingham. Queen Elizabeth I, eager to extend her glory, wealth and empire, encouraged many explorers to set sail for the New World in her name.

Henry Hudson

Scurvy, caused by a lack of the vitamin C present in fresh fruit and vegetables, wiped out many early voyages of exploration whose crews were dependent on dried and salted provisions. A simple but effective cure was found to be daily rations of fruit-juice.

John Davis followed, and mapped the rest of the coast of Baffin Island: the Davis Strait is named after him. His reports of the strait's rich sealing and whaling potential, and the abundance of cod off the Labrador coast, encouraged other expeditions to brave the Arctic.

In 1610, Henry Hudson sailed through another strait and entered what is now known as Hudson Bay. He had visited the New World before, naming and charting the Hudson River. When he realized that this river would not lead him to the Orient, he took his sloop *The Discovery* to the North.

Hudson and his men made good progress and were confident that they had found the way to the East. But as winter set in, they entered James Bay. During the winter the men had almost no fresh food. Scurvy broke out. The crew, bitter and desperate, turned on Hudson and the sick sailors and set them adrift in a small rowboat to die. The mutineers returned to England after terrible hardships, only to be cast in prison. Another attempt to find the passage had ended in miserable failure.

Still, men continued to challenge the cold and savage gales. In 1833 a British explorer, John Ross, and nineteen of his crew were discovered on Baffin Island, where they had been stranded without provisions for four years. They had survived by adopting the lifestyle of the native people who befriended them. Later explorers, among them Henry Larsen, were to prove that this is the surest method of surviving in the Arctic.

Other explorers preferred to take their means of survival with them. Twelve years after Ross returned to Britain, Sir John Franklin led an expedition by sea to link up with fur traders of the Hudson's Bay Company who had reached the Arctic by land. He was better equipped than any previous expedition had been: his ship was steam-powered and iron-clad to withstand the pressure of the ice, and he took with him enough provisions to last for three years. In spite of this preparation, Franklin and his crew disappeared, for many years without trace, and although the many ships that set out in search of Franklin did much to open up the seaways of the Arctic, the passage to the Orient remained elusive.

Finally, in 1903, the great Norwegian explorer Roald Amundsen, following as far as possible Franklin's course, passed through Ross Strait and berthed at Gjoa

Haven. He spent two long winters in the Arctic before the ice freed his vessel and allowed him to sail into the Pacific.

Another forty years passed before the little R.C.M.P. boat *St. Roch,* under the command of Sergeant Larsen, successfully completed the Northwest Passage. Although Amundsen was the first man to struggle through the passage, it was Larsen's achievements that showed the Arctic could really be used as the seaway dreamed of for so long. Besides taking the *St. Roch* through the passage in both directions, in over thirty years as captain of the *St. Roch* Larsen explored almost the entire Arctic. Most modern tankers use the deep-water route he pioneered in 1944. Every ship that sails the Northwest Passage owes its success in some part to Larsen and the *St. Roch.*

Sir John Franklin

Chapter 2 Early Days at Sea

In later years, one of Larsen's crew called him "a true Viking." Who were the Vikings, and why might Larsen be associated with them?

Henry Asbjorn Larsen was born in 1899 in Norway, near the Oslo Fiord. The sea almost surrounds Norway and Sweden, and has carved deep inlets into the heart of the land. The Scandinavians have always been seafarers, and many depend on the sea for their livelihood.

The ocean fascinated Henry Larsen from childhood. At first, during summer vacations, he would sail on the pilot boats. As soon as he was old enough, he did all kinds of work on fishing boats and pleasure craft. History and geography were his favourite subjects at school, and anything that touched on the polar lands and the great explorers was of particular interest.

Larsen was lucky enough to have a sympathetic teacher, who encouraged him to read books on these topics. It was here that Larsen first came across the names of Nansen and Amundsen. In later years, he would actually meet these great explorers.

When he was fifteen years old, Larsen signed to work on a ship owned by one of his uncles. The ship's only job was to carry lumber between Swedish and Norwegian ports. The work was drudgery, heavy and boring, but at least Larsen was on a ship, and he was happy. Soon he signed on the barque *Baunen*, bound for Florida out of London.

The First World War had broken out in 1914, and Larsen's ship arrived in London at the height of a German Zeppelin raid. Submarine attacks made any transatlantic voyage hazardous, but the *Baunen*'s crew were worked so hard they had no time to worry. Often Larsen and his friends would be kept busy for sixteen or twenty hours at a stretch. Their diet consisted mainly of salt meat, dried fish and hard biscuit. After swallowing mugs of canned milk, the men sometimes discovered a few cockroach corpses at the bottom of the can. It was not exactly a luxury cruise.

Shortly after arriving in the United States, Larsen transferred to another vessel that took him to South America. Like his other ships, this was a sailing craft. Although Larsen was at sea during the entire period of

the First World War, his ship was never attacked. He suffered storms, shipwreck and hurricane, but survived them all.

When the war came to an end in 1918, Larsen realized that if he was to advance in his profession, he must get further education. Returning to Norway, he entered navigation school. He graduated after two years, aged 21, qualified to navigate both steam and sailing ships anywhere in the world. By this time, the era of

Roald Amundsen, born only a short way from Henry Larsen's birthplace, was one of the greatest explorers of all. After conquering the Northwest Passage he went on to become the first man to reach the South Pole, in 1911, and made history again in 1926 when he made an airplane flight from Norway to Alaska, across the North Pole.

sailing vessels was almost over, but in spite of the regular hours and far better food on motorized craft, Larsen preferred to work on the stately sailing ships. He had a keen sense of the romance of the great age of sail and he stayed with the sailing ships for as long as possible. These took him all over the world: to South Africa, South America, Honolulu, the Orient and the west coast of Canada.

Finally in 1922, Larsen signed as fourth mate on the "Motor Ship" *Theodore Roosevelt,* and made four trips from Norway to the Pacific. It was on the third of these trips that he first saw the polar explorer Roald Amundsen. Returning to Norway, Larsen shared his cabin with Oscar Omdahl, who had piloted Amundsen's plane in the Arctic. The plane had been wrecked and Omdahl was returning home. On that long voyage Omdahl regaled Larsen with tales of the Arctic. Larsen was captivated, and his boyhood fascination with the Arctic was rekindled. He decided his future rested in the North, and made only one more trip before leaving his ship, bound for the Arctic.

Larsen had caught "Arctic Fever." The lure of almost unlimited space and the challenge of survival and discovery has drawn many men to the Far North, to test their endurance and ingenuity in the inhospitable conditions of the Arctic.

Larsen was soon able to answer the call. While reading a newspaper one day, he noticed that a Dane called Cristian Klengenberg had bought a schooner and wanted to hire a navigator for it. Larsen wasted no time in getting down to Seattle to apply for the position: this was the opportunity he had been waiting for. Larsen's knowledge and enthusiasm impressed Klengenberg, and he was hired as soon as he presented himself. His dreams of sailing into the Arctic were about to come true.

Herschel Island Chapter 3

Klengenberg's home was on Herschel Island, off the coast of the Yukon, and it was here that Larsen spent his first Arctic winter. For nine long months, the days were dark except for a few hours of twilight at mid-day, and the temperature fell as low as −40°C. Most people would have found this forced stay far from pleasant, but Larsen was fascinated by everything he saw and learned.

It was here that he began to acquire the knowledge of the Arctic that was to prove so valuable later. Above all, he got to know the Inuit people, with their humour, their generosity, and their skills. He received a good introduction to Inuit hospitality early in his stay on Herschel Island. Klengenberg's trip to buy the schooner had been quite an occasion, as it had been his first visit to the South in seventeen years. As a result, his Inuit

This stark landscape is typical of outposts in the Canadian Arctic.

friends and neighbours greeted his return with a series of non-stop parties. It was characteristic of the Inuit to celebrate almost any occasion with a good party. The eating, singing and tea-drinking lasted for days.

The Inuit are also great gift-givers, but Larsen was scarcely prepared for the first present offered him. A considerate Inuit woman, afraid that the newcomer Larsen might feel neglected since Klengenberg was guest of honour, rummaged around in a bag hanging from her waist. Suddenly she yanked out a juicy piece of blubber. She began to cut it into small chunks, licking it to clean it. When she was satisfied that it was clean, she offered it to Larsen. To refuse the gift would have been an insult. Larsen did not hesitate. He ate his portion with zest and smiled widely.

His diplomacy was again tested when he was offered something to eat that at first glance appeared to be a human hand. One of Klengenberg's sons quickly explained that it was in fact the flipper from a baby seal, and quite good eating. Larsen calmly consumed his portion.

The great popularity that Larsen was to acquire with the Inuit was partly due to the fact that he never appeared surprised at any of their customs. He accepted them with courtesy and without comment.

On Herschel Island, the Inuit taught Larsen some of the skills that enabled them to survive in the Arctic. First, he learned how to handle a dog team. He soon became adept, and found the dogs excellent workers if treated with a mixture of affection and discipline. To work efficiently, the dogs had to be well fed (they ate 3-4 kilograms of fish or meat a day), so the wise traveller always made sure that there was an ample supply of food for the dog team. While staying with Klengenberg, Larsen met the Danish explorer Knud Rasmussen, who had just completed a journey of thousands of kilometres from Greenland by dog team, proof of the amazing strength of the northern huskie.

Next came snow-shoeing. Larsen's first attempt, however, was almost a disaster. While trying to climb over a partially buried tree, he lost his footing and found himself suspended upside down, with his head in the snow. It was a dangerous predicament. Fortunately he was able to free himself before any serious damage had

Larsen looks a picture of confidence, but his early attempts at snowshoeing were disastrous.

Larsen proudly displays his catch — a huge seal.

been done, but after that incident he was always very careful when wearing snowshoes.

To survive, the Arctic traveller must be able to hunt, so Larsen set about mastering the art of seal hunting. He marvelled at the patience and determination of the Inuit hunters. Seals must breathe fresh air, and to do this they make holes in the ice and swim from one hole to another to breathe. The hole is frequently covered with snow and quite invisible to the hunter, but a dog can sniff out the hole and lead the hunter to it. Then the waiting begins. The slightest noise will frighten the seal away, so the hunter must stand motionless by the hole, his harpoon at the ready, waiting for the seal to return. This may take hours. If the seal does return, the hunter has only one chance to kill it. A swift downward thrust of the harpoon must strike the seal in a vital spot. If he is successful, the long wait is worthwhile because the hunter's family is assured of a supply of meat, clothing and oil.

Larsen had to try his hand at catching a seal. Partly through good luck, but also because he had learned his lesson well, his first seal was a prize catch, a monstrous 500 kilogram animal.

The time on Herschel passed swiftly. He made many friends, both among the Inuit and members of the Royal Canadian Mounted Police stationed on the Island. Determined to stay in the Arctic, Larsen was faced with the problem of finding suitable work that would enable him to do so. The answer was obvious: join the Mounted Police and apply for Arctic patrol.

Larsen decided to become a member of the world-famous police force. When he heard rumours that the Mounted Police were to build a police boat to serve the tiny settlements and outposts in the North, he was more determined than ever to become one of them.

Since the R.C.M.P. accepted only Canadian citizens, he would have to live in Canada for at least five years and acquire citizenship. Larsen was not deterred. If he became a member of the R.C.M.P. northern boat patrol, he could devote his life to his two great passions: the Arctic, and the sea.

Ice-fishing is another method of finding food.

Chapter 4 **The *St. Roch***

The St. Roch was the first R.C.M.P. boat specifically designed for Arctic patrol duties. The R.C.M.P. still maintains ships in the North, but many of the functions of the Arctic sea patrol have been taken over by aircraft, or by the Canadian Coastguard Service.

During most of the five years of waiting, Larsen served as navigator on Captain Klengenberg's two masted schooner *The Maid of Orleans*, sailing the Arctic seas. In the autumn of 1927, Larsen applied for Canadian citizenship. Shortly after the New Year of 1928 he applied to join the R.C.M.P., and after a few weeks he was accepted. Meanwhile, what had been rumoured for years finally came to pass. The R.C.M.P. were to have a vessel of their own for service in the Arctic. This was the opportunity that Larsen had been waiting for.

Larsen kept close watch on the new ship. It was built at the Burrard Shipyard in North Vancouver and was completed at the end of May, 1928. She was not a

particularly attractive ship but she was well suited for
the role she was to play. That was, to sail the Western
Arctic with supplies and medical assistance, and if
necessary, to remain in the ice over winter.

The vessel was 32 metres long with a beam of 8
metres. When fully laden she had a draft of about 4
metres. She was strongly built with a hull of Douglas fir,
sheathed on the outside with Australian ironbark to
resist the grinding pressure of ice floes. Special pressure
beams were installed to counteract the crushing force of
the ice, and the hull was rounded so the ship would tend
to bob up when the pressure of the ice was too great.
Unfortunately, the hull also had the effect of making the
ship roll violently — almost all the crew suffered
miserable bouts of seasickness. The *St. Roch* was
powered with a 150-horsepower diesel motor but
depended to a great extent on the three sails that she
carried.

The *St. Roch* was small and uncomfortable. The
captain's cabin was scarcely large enough for him to
dress in. The kitchen, or galley, was little more than a
closet, and unfortunately the cook was the largest
member of the crew.

Larsen's friend, Corporal E. Pasley, had been given
command of the new ship, but although he had some
experience in the Royal Navy, he knew nothing about
equipping a ship, especially one designed for Arctic
service. Indeed, with the exception of Henry Larsen, who
was posted to the *St. Roch* as an ordinary seaman, none
of the crew knew anything about the Arctic and only a
few had any sailing experience.

The ship was equipped with only one lifeboat and
that was far too heavy and clumsy. The *St. Roch* should
have had a light boat that could be easily and quickly
launched for seal-hunting and fishing. The anchor gear
was entirely unsatisfactory, and the engines underpowered because the designer had thought that most of
the time the ship would be under sail. The motors were
intended to be used only in emergencies.

Just before the *St. Roch* left on her maiden voyage,
Corporal Pasley resigned. The command was then given
to a young constable called Lamothe who was
unfamiliar with the Arctic and with sailing ships. As the
only man with any experience, Larsen was promoted to

This picture of the St. Roch's mess gives some indication of the cramped conditions aboard ship.

first mate and soon found he had to make all decisions concerned with seamanship.

Finally, at the end of June, the *St. Roch* set sail for the Arctic. As soon as she had left the protection of the harbour it became evident that the ship was not designed for comfort. To make matters worse, no sooner was she in the open sea when she was struck by a wind of gale proportions. The *St. Roch* pitched and rolled and the poor Mounted Police, who had never experienced anything like it before, quickly became seasick. It was just as well that no one felt like eating because a huge wave had swept into the galley and everything — eggs, bread, milk and flour — was mixed into one horrible mess. It was impossible to keep a fire going there, so those who did want to eat were forced to chew on biscuits and cold ham.

While conditions on this first voyage were far worse than they need have been, the crew seems to have accepted all inconveniences with good will. Larsen's expertise inspired confidence, and morale on the trip was high.

Captain Larsen's sternness was relieved by a ready sense of humour. Here he enters into the spirit of washday in the Arctic.

Finally the weather settled down — the one sure cure for seasickness. It was so calm that some of the crew fished for cod over the side of the boat. The catch was large and everyone looked forward to a good fish dinner after all the makeshift meals. Larsen, unable to go below to eat with the rest of the crew, was surprised to see them all dash up on deck looking slightly green and rush for the rail. The cook had boiled the fish whole without cutting off the heads and the men found it impossible to eat the fish with all those large eyes staring at them!

On her way north, the *St. Roch* stopped at an American port in Alaska. The crew were obeying their orders to wear the Mounties' uniform as often as possible during the voyage, although it was ill-suited to life aboard ship. The Americans were greatly surprised to see a ship's crew dressed smartly in tunics, striped pants and boots. Naturally, there was a lot of joking, but the Americans soon offered to make a number of minor repairs to the *St. Roch* which improved the comfort and efficiency of the ship considerably.

Scarcely had the *St. Roch* passed through the Bering Strait (which separates Alaska from the U.S.S.R.) and entered the Arctic Ocean when she ran into trouble.

Some of the navigation channels were improperly charted, and the ship ran aground. This was a common problem in the Arctic, and there were a number of standard methods for getting afloat. One way was to unload the entire cargo, in the hope that the ship would float off the shoal. This put the crew to a lot of trouble, and more often than not, the ship remained stranded. Alternatively, a wire cable would be fastened to some object on shore, and the ship pulled off the reef by windlass. If that too proved useless, there was nothing for it but to wait for a wind of sufficient strength to blow the ship into deep water. Fortunately, on this occasion, the *St. Roch* floated off the reef before too long.

After two months on board the *St. Roch*, Larsen was promoted to skipper. This was a striking tribute to his character, his experience and his ability. His crewmen at first thought him a stern disciplinarian, but they soon came to respect his expert seamanship and his experience in dealing with the hazards of Arctic navigation. Larsen was a quiet but effective leader, calm in the face of danger and always ready to seek advice. Those who knew him well found him to be a shy but humorous man, humble in spite of his achievements, and one who showed equal respect when talking to either a high-ranking official or a primitive northern hunter.

Henry Larsen enjoys the brief transformation that springtime brings·to Herschel Island.

Arctic Duties Chapter 5

To be made skipper and chief navigator of a ship was a great honour, especially after such a short time in the service. But Larsen possessed what no other Mountie had — experience. Larsen was responsible for all matters connected with seamanship, while the senior R.C.M.P. sergeant aboard was responsible for police matters. After five years Sergeant Anderton was posted to Ottawa and Larsen was given the sole command of the *St. Roch.* He sailed the boat safely through the Arctic for many years.

As the giant ice floes moved relentlessly on, driven by gale-force winds, there was always the danger that the little ship would be crushed by ice. The rounded hull came into its own here: ice floes that would have crushed the sides of a conventional ship slid harmlessly under the keel of the *St. Roch.* Though the ship would be hoisted several feet into the air, her weight would eventually break the ice, and she would settle back into the water. During Larsen's years with the *St. Roch* various improvements were made to the ship, but two basic faults were never overcome: her excessive rolling in even moderate seas and her cramped accommodation.

Once fire came close to destroying the *St. Roch.* The smell of smoke alerted the crew, but the engine was going at full speed, and could not be reached because of the heat. Right beside the flames was a keg holding three hundred pounds of blasting powder, enough to blow the *St. Roch* to splinters. Larsen managed to secure a fire extinguisher and put out the flames, but the incident was a reminder that danger was a constant companion. Survival itself was a struggle in the cruelly harsh Arctic climate. The crew of the *St. . Roch* had not only to survive, but also to provide an efficient police patrol in the Arctic waters.

Sailing between the various settlements and police posts, it was the *St. Roch's* duty to maintain order in Canada's Arctic Islands and Northwest Territories. This involved maintaining game-laws and conveying the young to school and the sick to hospital.

One important duty was to assist the treatment of

Larsen called the St. Roch "the
most uncomfortable ship" he had
ever sailed in. The flattened hull
made the ship roll badly, but
enabled her to ride up over ice
which would have crushed any
other vessel.

epidemics in Inuit settlements. Since the Inuit had practically no resistance to our diseases, it was not uncommon for entire families to be wiped out by illnesses, such as influenza or measles, which seem fairly harmless to us. Unfortunately, the Inuit who ran a high fever would strip to the skin and sit outside to cool off. Pneumonia and death almost invariably followed. When an epidemic broke out, the most important thing was to keep it from spreading. This meant leaving a constable in charge of the settlement to enforce quarantine.

Broken bones and gunshot wounds were common among the native people. When the Mounted Police heard of an accident, the patient was collected and taken to the nearest hospital, which might be hundreds of kilometres away.

Enforcing the law was a task Larsen sometimes found distasteful. The official Canadian law often conflicted with native beliefs and customs, and crimes were committed because the native people did not fully understand the new law. In such harsh surroundings with the possibility of death always present, the Inuit did not regard some murders as seriously as the police patrols did. Depending on the circumstances, punishment was often very light. When murder had been committed, the accused might have to be taken a great distance to be tried before a judge. It was not unusual for the *St. Roch* to transport an accused murderer, his family and his dogs for hundreds of kilometres in very bad conditions.

Larsen's patrol duties often took him back to Herschel Island, where he could visit his old friends, in particular Klengenberg. As time passed, he saw many changes in the islanders' way of life.

Many years before, Herschel Island had been a rendezvous for whalers, but as the whales dwindled in number the island lost much of its importance, and for a few years it was inhabited solely by a few Inuit and the birds of many species that nest there.

More recently, the island has regained much of its importance. In the 1920s, oil was discovered in parts of the Arctic. At first, the cost of training men and designing equipment to work in Arctic conditions seemed prohibitive, but soon came the realization that the world's more accessible supplies of oil were running

The drilling ships and supertankers now based in the Arctic need a deepwater port. To build one would cost millions of dollars. Extensive development of the natural harbour on Herschel would wipe out many rare species of birds which nest there. Which is more important, the development of sources of energy, or the preservation of wildlife?

Four modes of transportation meet. The St. Roch *and her team of huskies meet their more modern competitors, the snowmobile and the airplane.*

out. The Arctic became an area of strategic importance.
Herschel Island's natural deepwater harbour at Pauline
Cove became a busy port again, but the whale-boats
were replaced by floating laboratories, drilling-ships and
large tankers.

In the days of Henry Larsen's patrols, the problems of
developing modern industries in the Arctic were just
becoming apparent. The R.C.M.P. were especially concerned with the effects that modern North American and
European civilization would have on the traditional way
of life of the Inuit. One of the Mounties' most important
duties was to protect the native people from exploitation.

Although newspapers were occasional luxuries in the Arctic, Larsen was an avid reader, mainly of books on science and exploration, and he had plenty of time for his hobby when his ship was frozen fast in the ice.

The Overland Patrols
Chapter 6

The *St. Roch* patrolled the Arctic between 1928 and 1948, and often spent long periods — even entire winters — trapped in the ice.

The worst of the winter storms forced Larsen and his crew to stay on board the *St. Roch,* but they fared quite well. The intense cold froze their provisions just as a modern freezer does. Potatoes, oranges, lemons, eggs and meat were preserved in this way, and could be thawed when necessary by dropping them into boiling water.

The seamen remained cheerful while the ice creaked and roared outside. Blinding blizzards could be whipped up by the wind in a matter of minutes, and towering ice floes threatened to crush the *St. Roch.* From the windswept vantage point of the crow's nest, the captain kept a look-out for cracks, or "leads", that offered a short relief from the pressure of the ice.

One of Larsen's customs was to sing hymns while he stood watch. The louder the storm roared, the louder Larsen sang. One of the constables in Larsen's crew had this to say:

The skipper was well known, well liked, but above all well respected both by Inuit and White. Of course he had his share of curious customs. One of them was to stand on deck during a violent gale and sing hymns at the top of his voice. Now sailors are a superstitious lot and this hymn singing didn't go down well. But it was a sight to see his short, stocky figure standing there as though he was daring the Arctic to do its worst.

When the weather improved, however, Larsen and his crew took advantage of the snows of winter to make lengthy overland patrols by dogsled. As his ability to handle the dogs improved, so did the length of his patrols; during his years in the Arctic, Larsen visited most of the settlements of the Arctic Peninsula.

Larsen was fortunate in finding for his team a lead dog of unusual intelligence. The dog, on his own, was able to find the best spot for setting up camp. It would keep the other dogs in order, and often at night it would be seen circling the camp, just as a human sentry might do. Such a lead dog was a valuable asset: without a strong leader a team would become disorganized, tangling the harness in seconds. In bitterly cold weather it could take hours to untangle it.

Under suitable conditions, a team could cover 80 kilometres a day. The sleighs used on these journeys were about five metres long and could carry up to seven hundred kilograms of supplies.

If Larsen and his companions did not wish to be burdened with a tent they would make a small igloo for the night's rest. With a sharp knife and a good supply of hard snow, a good-sized igloo can be built in about an hour. The fault of the igloo is not that it is too cold, but rather that it gets too hot. Body heat and a small cooking stove can easily cause the roof to melt and collapse on the people inside. Larsen became adept at making igloos, but used a piece of canvas as the roof to prevent collapse.

One of the first duties every morning was to melt snow in order to coat the runners of the sled with a thin film of ice. This reduced friction, enabling the sleighs to slide easily over the rough snow.

Food on these patrols could sometimes be procured by shooting caribou or seal. Arctic hare and ptarmigan also provided excellent eating. On shorter patrols or when time could not be spared to go hunting, the Mounties would take along food prepared beforehand.

One of the most tasty and nourishing dishes that Larsen concocted was a kind of stew. Two or three kilograms of beans were put in a big pot, to which were added a quantity of finely chopped bacon, some tomatoes, onions, molasses, sugar, mustard and salt. The whole stew was left to simmer until it became thick, when it was taken out of the pot and allowed to freeze in large pans. The frozen stew was then cut into small cubes. On a patrol, the men could quickly prepare a meal by putting a few cubes of the frozen stew in a pot of water or tomato juice. In a short time the stew would be completely thawed and ready to eat. Almost any combination of meat, rice and potatoes could be dealt with in a similar way. These pre-packed meals were very nourishing, and importantly, took up very little room on the sled

The crew haul aboard a captured walrus. Game provided a welcome addition to their diet of frozen and canned food.

Instead of loaves of bread, which took up too much space, hundreds of doughnuts were prepared beforehand. On the trail these frozen doughnuts would be put on the lid of the stew-pot while it was heating up. By the time it was ready to eat, the doughnuts were thawed too.

Frozen fish slices provided another useful, quick source of food.

"Strange as it seems" wrote Larsen, "raw, frozen fish gives one a warm feeling of well-being after a few minutes. The natives say that the frozen fish forces the warm blood from the inside out to the skin and makes one feel warm. This sounds reasonable to me as I have tried it many times."

Larsen's readiness to adopt Inuit customs not only ensured his survival in the Arctic (they were, after all, experts at surviving there), but also endeared him to the Inuit themselves. Larsen admired the endurance and good humour with which they withstood harsh conditions, and they in turn responded with friendship and respect: "Henry with the big ship" was a welcome visitor throughout the Arctic.

Larsen made great friends with the Inuit, who called him Hanorie Umiarjuaq, Henry with the Big Ship.

The Inuit Chapter 7

Larsen's travels throughout the North brought him into
close contact with the Inuit, the natives of the Arctic.
Apart from his professional duties, Larsen was
interested in every aspect of the Inuit's culture and life-
style. He was an observant man, he had won the
friendship of the Inuit and he understood their difficult
language. Few men have spent so much time with the
Inuit or have come to know them so well. His accounts
of his travels contain many fascinating insights and
anecdotes concerning the isolated inhabitants of the Far
North.

One of the first things Larsen discovered was that the
natives were to be called *Inuit* and not *Eskimos.* Inuit
means "The People" while *Eskimo* is the name given
them by the Cree Indians and was intended as an insult.
Eskimo means "eater of raw meat." The Inuit do
occasionally eat flesh and blubber raw (when it is more
nutritious) and with good reason: it is often impossible
to make a fire in the wind and snow, and when meat and
fish freeze hard as soon as they are caught, there is little
danger that they will perish or become poisoned.

Today, instead of depending on dogs for transportation, the *Inuk,* or Inuit man, travels by snowmobile.
Instead of sitting motionless for hours by a hole in the ice
waiting for a seal to appear, he may work for an oil
company, earn high wages in a short time and buy his
food off the shelves of a grocery store. His shanty-home
of skins or driftwood (the igloo was usually used only as
a temporary dwelling on hunting trips) has been
replaced by a more substantial cabin, often built by the
government, which also provides medical care and
education.

In many ways, the hard life of the Inuit has been
made easier, but civilization came to them suddenly, and
it was a mixed blessing. As the native people came into
contact with North Americans and Europeans, their
desire for modern possessions increased, though many
of these goods were inappropriate to their traditional
way of life. When the Inuit, used to hunting with

Tradition meets modernization in the Arctic: the Inuit still build igloos, but the sled is supplemented by the ski-doo.

harpoons and arrows, first received rifles, they cele-brated by shooting indiscriminately, amazed at the ease with which game could be killed. For a while the caribou and seal were in danger of being wiped out, but with the assistance of the R.C.M.P., hunting controls were established to protect and maintain the wildlife vital to the Inuit's existence.

When Henry Larsen first visited the Arctic, the Inuit still led a primitive life. Imagine the difficulties: the temperature remains well below zero for much of the year, and even if the snow disappears only a very thin layer of ground ever thaws, so agriculture is impossible. Apart from a few summer berries, the Inuit must live entirely on the game they catch. There are virtually no trees, so the only wood available for making houses, sleds or weapons is drift-wood. The Inuit must use bone, soapstone or skins, and even occasionally make sleds from frozen fish or meat slices. In winter, there is almost darkness, and swarms of mosquitoes and blackflies have been known to cause large animals to stampede to death.

Before the coming of the traders, caribou and seal were the key to survival in the Arctic. They provided food that could be frozen and kept for months, their hides provided warm clothing, their fat was used for food, heat and light, and tools and weapons were carved from their bones and antlers. It is easy to understand why the killing of a caribou or seal was cause for a celebration.

Traditionally, the man was the hunter while the woman stayed with the children, did the cooking and made the clothing. By far the best clothing for comfort and protection from the cold is made from caribou-skin. Larsen's crew on Arctic patrol preferred native caribou sleeping-sacks to those provided by the R.C.M.P.

The clothing produced by the Inuit women appears deceptively careless. In fact, a great deal of skill goes into the making of a suit, which may take ten pelts, and is carefully tailored so that loss of body heat is slight. A suit is usually two pelts thick with the fur of the first pelt on the inside next to the body, and the fur of the second skin on the outside. In the past, the furs were stitched together with animal-sinew thread, using goose or gull wingbone needles.

Carving is no longer a necessity for the Inuit, but it has become very profitable. Carvings such as this are highly prized in the South.

Carving was a traditional Inuit craft and pastime. Before traders brought superior iron and steel implements, the Inuit carved weapons and tools from bones, tusks and antlers. Modern carvings are of animals, hunters, fishermen and family groups. For this purpose the Inuit find that soapstone is more satisfactory than the traditional materials, which are now in short supply. With their smooth, graceful lines, Inuit carvings are prized as some of the most beautiful examples of native art in the world.

Larsen was interested in all the traditional skills of the Inuit, but he feared that they were in danger of dying out. He often noted that relics of ancient tribes who had inhabited the North suggested that these tribes were more advanced than the Inuit he knew. Their ivory ornaments and weapons were more finely carved. The Inuit of the Boothia Peninsula talk about the people who lived there before them, a tall race, called the Tunit People. They lived in houses built around whale-ribs, so

A group of Inuit explore the "Big Ship" with interest.

they must have hunted these large mammals successfully. Larsen regrets the fact that so little is known about the origins of the Inuit. He writes,

Their legends, old beliefs and customs are dying out fast; the bringers of civilization have been too busy teaching them our history, beliefs and ways of living to find out anything about these people first. They are one of the most remarkable peoples in the world today.

His own first hand experience of the difficulty of survival in the Artic taught Larsen to respect the good-natured endurance of the Inuit. They seemed to remain calm and even cheerful in the face of great hardship. This cheerfulness has puzzled many explorers, but the Inuit have an explanation: "If you knew the horrors we often have to live through, you would understand why we are so fond of laughing."

The Inuit had over a hundred words for different types of snow, but none for war. They had no time for war, since it was a struggle simply to stay alive. Survival depended on co-operation and decisions were taken by groups and not by any single leader. Larsen always noticed that families were very close, sharing homes, food, pleasures and troubles.

Acts of heroism and self-sacrifice were not infrequent. Larsen recalls an incident involving an Inuit called Old Adam.

Old Adam had been out hunting with his grandson when a sudden blizzard blew up. They could go no further. The snow was not suitable for building an igloo, so all they could do was scoop a hole in the snow on the ground. There the two lay huddled for days. When the storm subsided, their family and friends set out in search of the two lost ones. They were soon found, but Old Adam was dead. To save his grandson, he had made him wear most of his clothing and had covered the boy's body with his own.

When an Inuit becomes too feeble to help support his family and knows that he will be nothing but a burden to them by eating their precious food, he will sometimes leave the igloo and disappear forever. The R.C.M.P. have curbed this custom to some extent, and trade with the South means that survival is not as hard as it once was, but Larsen recognized the courage of this act of self-sacrifice.

To relieve the harshness of their daily life, the Inuit were always ready to celebrate, and Larsen, though a shy man, shared this love for parties.

At Christmas, 1935, he and his men planned a surprise for the natives. The Inuit had never heard of Santa Claus, so for days the Mounties talked of nothing but Santa's coming on Christmas Eve.

When the day arrived, over three hundred Inuit had gathered. The night was clear and cold as all waited for Santa's arrival. Suddenly there was a loud bang in the sky, followed by thousands of small stars. Out of the dark came a red-coated figure with a bushy red beard. The Inuit turned and fled, but it was not long before they realized it was their friend, Henry Larsen. When the Mounties started handing out presents any lingering fear vanished. Dinner followed, consisting of stew, biscuits and tea laden with sugar, and the party continued almost non-stop until New Year.

Once Larsen, dressed in his colourful uniform, visited an Inuit family. His buttons, polished till they shone, attracted an elderly Inuit lady. Nothing would do but she must marry Larsen. He could not conceal his dismay and surprise. In the meantime the rest of the family had collapsed in gales of laughter. Larsen, already happily married, avoided the proposal, but the story became a classic in the Arctic.

Chapter 8 The Northwest Passage

In the spring of 1940, Sergeant Larsen was summoned to Ottawa to appear before Commissioner S.T. Wood, senior officer of the R.C.M.P. Larsen was a modest man, and his account of this meeting is characteristically understated: "We then received one of our most important, and to my mind most interesting, assignments. Our Commissioner informed us that when our regular duties were completed we were to proceed to Halifax, N.S., by the way of the Northwest Passage."

Under Larsen's command the *St. Roch* had performed admirable service supplying the Western Arctic R.C.M.P. outposts. Now he was to attempt a voyage that would make him a celebrity. This meant little to Larsen. Of greater importance was the fact that he would be able to follow the route of so many great explorers, safely accomplished by only one — Amundsen. No one had ever before sailed the passage from west to east. Larsen accepted the challenge with enthusiasm. His years in the Arctic had been an ideal preparation for this great adventure.

Canada was at war in 1940 and could ill afford to spare either men or materials unless absolutely necessary. But the government realized that Canada's claim to the Arctic could only be maintained if it was regularly visited and patrolled.

The Arctic Archipelago, that is all the land that lay north of continental Canada to the North Pole, was several million square kilometres in extent. Canada did not intend to stand idly by and watch other nations lay claim to all or part of it. In the nineteenth century there had been incursions by other nations into the area and it was for this reason that the Prime Minister, Sir Wilfrid Laurier, had sent Captain Bernier to claim the land for Canada.

Now, in 1940, with the war spreading all over the world, it seemed wise to reassert Canada's sovereignty,

In his early days as skipper of the St. Roch, Constable Larsen was heard to ask a visiting inspector for permission to sail through the Eastern Arctic. The Inspector brushed the request aside. In 1940, however, Larsen's orders were quite clear: "Take her to Halifax, over the top." By now a seasoned Arctic traveller, Larsen was ready for the challenge.

Who could do it better than the Mounted Police in the force's own ship? In 1904, the first Mountie detachment had been stationed at Herschel Island, and ever since then, a handful of men had maintained the law in that huge area.

It was to be expected that in wartime everything would be in short supply. However, the mission was so important and time so short that most necessary repairs were done quickly. Depending on the ice conditions, Larsen hoped to make the voyage with one stop for winter. But the *St. Roch* had scarcely left Vancouver when it was found that the clutch machinery needed fixing.

The ship had to return to port. The repairs did not take long and once again Larsen set out, only to find that the fuel pump was not working. This time it was not necessary to return to Vancouver. The pump was repaired at a small harbour up the coast, but the repairs took time, and because the season when it was possible to sail in the Arctic was so short, a few days could make an enormous difference to the success or failure of a voyage.

It had been decided to sail the southern route, which would take them through Queen Maud Gulf, south of King William Island, then north between the Boothia Peninsula and Somerset Island, finally skirting the north coast of Baffin Island to Halifax. During the course of the voyage, the Mounted Police had to carry out their regular duties: indeed, when the *St. Roch* set sail from Vancouver she was so laden with supplies that it was difficult to see the deck. Hundreds of sacks of coal, drums of oil, crates of eggs, potatoes and vegetables, small rowboats and scores of other packages were piled high everywhere.

At first the *St. Roch* made good time. There was a steady swell and the ship rolled as usual. The newcomers were seasick but the weather was by no means bad and the ship took advantage of it. Larsen, as always, paid tribute to his crew: "to their everlasting credit they stood up well; and soon found their sea-legs."

Though it was still July when they reached Point Barrow, the ice was already beginning to build up. Larsen did not want to be caught in an exposed position, because forecasts indicated that this would be a bad year

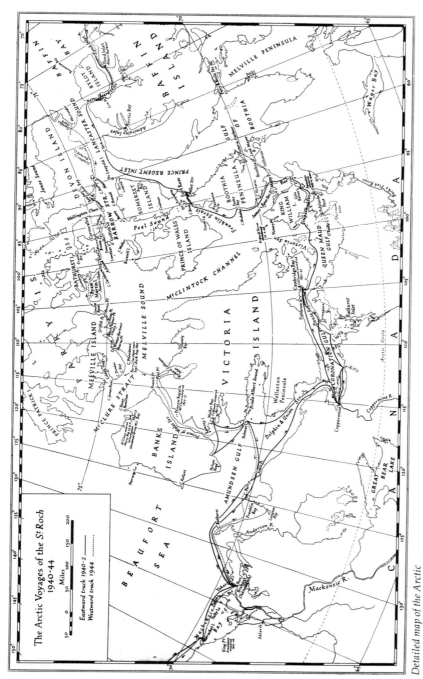

*Detailed map of the Arctic
showing the routes followed by
Henry Larsen.
The Canadian Government later
named the stretch of water
between McClintock Channel
and Boothia Peninsula, Larsen
Sound.*

for ice. The *St. Roch* persevered against strong, steady north winds, but it took twenty days to make the 650 km trip from Point Barrow to Herschel Island. Less than 40 kilometres a day is very slow going.

The first lot of supplies were to be put ashore at Herschel Island. The Hudson's Bay Post had by now moved to a settlement near the Mackenzie River Delta called Tuktoyaktuk, "the place where the deer cross", usually shortened to Tuk Tuk.

By September it was easy to see that there would be no trip to the Atlantic that year. Larsen decided to anchor in Prince of Wales Strait. This fairly central location offered some protection from the ice. Once the decision to winter here had been reached, there was a great deal to be done. A vitally important job was to catch enough fish to feed the dogs until the following spring, so nets were set in every lake that had not yet frozen over.

To make sure there was a plentiful supply of fresh water, huge blocks of ice in the fresh water lakes had to be cut and hauled to the ship. Almost 40 metric tons of ice were hauled aboard. Once winter set in, every drop of water used had to be melted. A full kettle was kept on the stove 24 hours a day.

Another job was to build a canvas tent over the ship so that fine snow would not sift into the living and sleeping quarters.

During the long winter months, the *St. Roch* was scraped, painted and given a complete overhaul. The Mounties made long patrols to inland settlements, taking a census of the Inuit population.

It was not until July 31, 1941 that the *St. Roch* was able to sail again. Once again as she headed eastward, bad ice conditions prevented her from making any speed. Finally Larsen returned to Tuk Tuk to take on fresh supplies both for the ship and the R.C.M.P. posts.

Conditions steadily worsened, and the ship was unable to complete the distance Larsen had hoped for in August and September. Attempting to sail through the James Ross Strait, the *St. Roch* was trapped by the ice and whipped by blinding snow squalls. The full force of the northwest gales was funnelled down McClintock Channel and flung huge ice floes against the *St. Roch.* The area was notorious for its shoals; if the ship were driven onto one of these and became wedged, she would be crushed completely.

Throughout the night, captain and crew waited helplessly as the ice floes crashed against *St. Roch*, but the ship's builders had designed her well. Although she pitched and rolled to an alarming degree, she withstood the pounding of the ice. When morning came the crew could see the icefield stretching from horizon to horizon, but the *St. Roch* still floated completely unharmed.

Taking advantage of every crack in the ice and sometimes using explosives to blast a way through, the *St. Roch* moved slowly northeast towards the Atlantic. By September, however, it was obvious that Larsen and his crew would have to spend another winter in the Arctic. They were badly disappointed: another year would have to be spent away from families and friends, and of course there was no certainty that the ship would make Halifax even in the following year.

While hopes of completing the voyage that year were abandoned, Larsen was determined to make as much progress as possible before the *St. Roch* became trapped for the winter. By September 11 they had worked their way north as far as Pasley Bay, near the Magnetic Pole, and here all progress was stopped by ice. It was August, 1942, before the *St. Roch* was able to move out of the bay.

In spite of the many close calls and dangers on the voyage, the crew was fortunate in remaining free from accident or illness. The only sad occurrence was the sudden and totally unexpected death from heart failure of Constable Albert ("Frenchy") Chartrand, while the *St. Roch* was wintering at Pasley Bay.

Since Chartrand had been Roman Catholic, the crew felt it would be proper for him to be buried by a minister of his faith. The closest Roman Catholic mission was at Pelly Bay, some 650 km away. In the dead of winter, Larsen and Corporal Patrick Hunt set out on the 1,300 kilometre journey. Both men had learned the way of life of the Arctic so well that they made the trip without difficulty.

The speed of a good dog team is quite remarkable. Day in and day out, without any special exertion, it can cover 80 kilometres. Larsen and Hunt, however were in no great hurry and took advantage of this trip to visit as many Inuit settlements as possible on the way. Wherever

Dressed in furs, with his sled laden, Larsen sets off on one of his extensive patrols inland.

This Inuit grandmother from Gjoa Haven remembered Amundsen who wintered there in 1903-4 and 1905-6.

they went, their arrival was the occasion for a big party, so the two Mounties did not make as much speed as they might have.

At the parties the visitors were guests of honour and were always given the most prized tidbits. This could be disconcerting. Larsen recalls the soup-pots, "some of which contained heads of large bearded seals, with long drooping moustaches and large mournful eyes staring at us from the pot." Their hostesses always insisted on licking the choicest morsels clean before offering them to the policemen, and as neither wished to refuse such well-meaning kindness both smilingly accepted the offerings.

At one of the settlements they visited, Larsen and Hunt met with Canon John Turner, an Anglican minister who had come from England, landed on Baffin Island was making his way slowly across the Arctic. He was a huge man, all the more impressive because he wore snow-white bearskins. The canon played the concertina at church services, which delighted the Inuit, so that he must play on and on until his arms ached. The Mounties arrived during a church service, just in time for the inevitable feast, to which they contributed tea and sugar and the use of their primus stoves. The two policemen also used this opportunity to get on with their work, and took a census.

Canon Turner provided Larsen and Hunt with a guide who took them to Father Henri, the Roman Catholic missionary. Father Henri had come from France and lived in one of the few stone houses in the Arctic. He had built it entirely by himself, matching the boulders and cementing them together with great skill. His appearance, too,was impressive, very tall and strong, with a bushy red beard. Father Henri shared the diet and life-style of the Inuit. "The respect and devotion the Inuit showed him was the testimony to his ability to live off the land," said Larsen. Father Henri readily agreed to conduct the burial service for "Frenchy" Chartrand.

The Mounted Police had arrived at Easter and, with about 80 Inuit, attended the Good Friday and Easter Day services. Afterwards came the celebration — Father Henri had kept an eye on the cooking pot during mass. He encouraged the Inuit to practise their ancestral skills, so the day ended with archery and harpoon competitions. Larsen and Hunt arranged prizes of tobacco, snow-glasses, tea and sugar for the winners, but found that everyone expected a prize. The Inuit reasoned that since everyone did as well as he possibly could, everyone deserved the same reward.

Larsen and Hunt arrived back at the *St. Roch* after a round trip of 71 days. A few weeks later, Father Henri came, as he had promised, and held the funeral service for "Frenchy" Chartrand. He was buried on the shore overlooking the bay, and his friends erected a large cairn and a cross to mark the grave. In gratitude to Father Henri, they gave him a beautiful teak cross for his mission.

The months passed quickly and, with the coming of August, the weather grew warmer. Everyone hoped that this time they would complete their voyage to the Atlantic.

Chapter 9 **Success**

The *St. Roch* had been icebound in Pasley Bay for eleven months. When she was finally able to head for the open sea in August, 1942, she was quickly beset by new dangers. At the end of August the ship was nearly lost in Bellot Strait. The strait was less than a kilometre wide and the current, forced into this narrow channel, was so violent that it flung the underpowered *St. Roch* around like a wood-chip, dashing her repeatedly against the ice. If she had sunk, the men would have died instantly in the icy water.

Trapped in ice, August 1942.

Two Inuit passengers thought that in this extremity they should try to help. They stood on the forecastle singing hymns with all their might. Larsen, who had been known to do the same thing himself, was amused. "They told me they were singing so the ship wouldn't get crushed, so I told them to keep on singing. They were quite pleased after we got through, when I told them their singing had no doubt helped us a great deal."

Sometimes the pressure of the ice floes around the *St. Roch* heaved the ship up into the air, so that she was in danger of capsizing. Charges of gunpowder were set off as close to the hull as safety permitted, to crack the ice and reduce the pressure.

Another threat was the possibility that both the propeller and rudder would become frozen solid. The crew had to keep constantly chipping away the ice. Sergeant Larsen never showed his concern, but at this time confided to his diary his fears that more than once the vessel seemed doomed.

On August 10, just when some progress was being made, one of the cylinders blew and the engine room was flooded. Immediately the men set about repairing the damage and did as good a job as possible in the circumstances, but there was no way to repair a broken cylinder while at sea so the *St. Roch* had to limp along for the rest of the way at eight kilometres an hour.

Larsen and his crew felt that when they had passed through Bellot Strait, the worst of the journey was over. The Hudson's Bay Company ship came this far from the east every year so the men on the *St. Roch* felt it would be easy sailing for them.

But very little is easy in the Arctic. In Davis Strait the sea was studded with small icebergs and "growlers" — small, submerged icebergs that could bob up like sea monsters, and though small, were capable of putting a hole clean through the *St. Roch* if they surfaced in the wrong spot. With such low power, it was difficult to dodge the "growlers" and still maintain some speed.

At last, when everything seemed to be going wrong, good luck came in the shape of a strong northerly gale. The gale struck on August 24, and such was the strength of the winds that the ice was soon shattered. The vessel had almost completely clear sailing and was able to proceed at full speed — eight kilometres an hour!

Larsen still respected the floating ice, but steadily progressed on the last leg of his journey.

At the beginning of September, having passed through the Arctic Ocean, Henry Larsen put into Pond Inlet to the north of Baffin Island. There the remainder of the stores of food and clothes were unloaded and the dogs put ashore. It was a sad parting.

It seemed, however, that the elements refused to let the *St. Roch* escape their grasp. All the way down the coasts of Baffin Island and Labrador one storm after another buffeted the ship.

On September 22, *St. Roch* put into Bateau Harbour in Newfoundland. Larsen and his crew had sailed from the Pacific to the Atlantic through the Northwest Passage. The voyage had taken 28 months.

The Second World War still raged in Europe and Asia, and little fuss was made over the *St. Roch*'s historic trip. But the voyage did not go unrecognized. To honour the men who had successfully sailed the Arctic, King George VI approved the award of the Polar Medal to Sergeant Larsen and the eight members of his crew. One of the eight was Constable Albert Chartrand.

Grim-faced, Larsen guides his wooden ship through the perils of an icy sea.

Chapter 10 **Back to Vancouver**

The world was at war, Sergeant Larsen and the crew of *St. Roch* were still on duty and for the rest of 1943 they were on antisubmarine patrol in the North Atlantic. German submarines were a constant threat in those waters but the *St. Roch* never met one. Actually, the greatest enemy was boredom and one crewman after another found some pretext to leave for a more varied and exciting life.

Finally in the summer of 1944, Henry Larsen was given new orders; he was instructed to bring the *St. Roch* back to Vancouver, once again by the Northwest Passage, this time by the northern route which had never before been navigated. Larsen set to work at once to prepare for the voyage. He managed to secure a diesel engine, larger and far more powerful than the original one, and supervised much needed changes in the ventilation system.

By far the most important task was to procure a new crew, no easy matter with the country at war. Almost every able-bodied man was active in some capacity connected with the war effort. At last, Larsen succeeded in recruiting a full crew, inexperienced, but willing to endure the hardships of the voyage in order to accompany Sergeant Larsen on his historic trip.

On July 22, 1944, the *St. Roch* set out from Halifax to attempt the Northwest Passage, this time sailing west. Just as she had done three years before in the Pacific, almost as soon as the *St. Roch* had left port, she ran into serious trouble. The new ventilation system was not working properly, and the pipes had become so hot that the tar on deck was beginning to bubble. There was a danger of fire breaking out so the ship returned at once to Sydney, Nova Scotia.

Fortunately the trouble was easily and quickly remedied and once again the *St. Roch* headed westward. The next problem concerned provisions. Larsen had by

In 1944, after sixteen years of continuous duty, the St. Roch *was in no shape to make a record-breaking trip. Her rig, that of an auxiliary schooner of the 20s, was outdated, and Larsen had to battle against wartime priorities to persuade navy officials to re-rig her as a ketch. They also installed five spartan cabins and a closed-in wheelhouse.*

great good fortune acquired a number of cases of beef stew. At a time when food was strictly rationed, this was indeed a prize, and would prove a savoury alternative to the fish and caribou they hoped to catch. To their disappointment, the first time the stew was served, the crew found that so much salt had been added at the cannery, that the stew was unfit to eat.

The weather was miserable, with persistent fog and freezing rain. Near the Labrador coast the *St. Roch* was hampered by ice floes and icebergs. To avoid them, Larsen was forced to follow the coast of Greenland for a

while. At last, the weather turned fair and they were able to sail through open water.

On August 12, they anchored at the R.C.M.P. post at Pond Inlet, where they unloaded some supplies and took aboard an Inuit, his wife, family and seventeen dogs. The family of seven pitched a tent on top of the deckhouse and lived there quite comfortably till they reached Herschel Island. The dogs suffered as the spray froze on them, so a makeshift kennel was built and, huddled together, they were quite happy.

With a stronger motor and much more ice-free water

"Never before," wrote Larsen, "had anyone prepared so badly for an Arctic voyage." Two of his crew were almost 70, the youngest was only 16. The wireless operator had never sent or received a message. They are shown here on July 22, 1944, the day the ship left Halifax bound for Vancouver.

on the northern route, the *St. Roch* made very good time on the return voyage, but gales and bad weather conditions still threatened the ship. Larsen recalls only one day of clear weather during the whole voyage. Snowstorms often made visibility poor, and with sonar equipment not yet invented, the *St. Roch*'s crew avoided running aground by taking constant soundings with a lead weight on a chain. While crossing the Lancaster Sound the ship ran into southeasterly gales which raised a dangerously choppy sea. The *St. Roch* cruised back and forth for six hours in the lee of a huge iceberg, while the vessel became covered with a sheet of ice from the spray and sleet.

When the storm abated, the *St. Roch* anchored in Dundas Harbour, Devon Island, while the crew went ashore and built a cairn to mark their progress. In it they put a brass cylinder containing the details of their expedition: the ship, its nationality, the date, and the names of captain and crew.

The *St. Roch* made her way westward, taking advantage of leads in the ice whenever they appeared. In Melville Sound, pack ice once again threatened to imprison the *St. Roch*, but by staying close to the south shores of the string of islands, Devon, Bathurst and Melville, she was able to make steady progress. The crew visited as many places of interest as time would allow, and built cairns to record the *St. Roch*'s visits, once again confirming that this territory was under control of the Canadian government.

At the entrance to McClure Strait, the *St. Roch* was sailing through waters that had never before been explored. Heavy ice held up progress, and thick fog and sleet caused Larsen to lose his way on one occasion, and sail into a narrow inlet by mistake.

Finally, the *St. Roch* turned down Prince of Wales Strait to be greeted by a day of brilliant sunshine. There, on September 4, the *St. Roch* met up with the *Fort Ross*, a Hudson's Bay Company boat which had left Halifax three months earlier, sailed south through the Panama Canal, and up the Pacific Coast. Together, the two Canadian boats had encircled the North American continent.

The ship was still making good progress, so Larsen decided to push on to Tuk Tuk. The *St. Roch* was now

This stamp was issued in 1978 to commemorate the voyages of the St. Roch.

approaching familiar territory, but there was no warm welcome in store. Strong winds piled ice against the ship, forcing it inshore, while a blinding snowstorm reduced visibility. Soon the snow gave way to fog which joined with the ice, as though deliberately trying to obstruct the boat's progress. All Larsen could do was tie up to the ice and wait for conditions to improve.

At last the *St. Roch* was able to move on, but it was dusk of September 8 by the time Tuk Tuk was sighted. With warnings of gale-force winds approaching, the *St. Roch* had to reach the safety of the harbour, but the bouys marking dangerous shallows were invisible in the darkness. The seas were already rough and the *St. Roch* pitched violently. At one point she ran aground on the shoals, but was able to free herself and enter the harbour, by what Larsen called a miracle, but the "miracle" was due largely to his own navigational skills.

The *St. Roch* reached safety just in time. Tuk Tuk was hit by the worst storm that had ever struck the settlement, with hurricane winds and severe floods. Goods and equipment were washed away and many dogs were drowned. Securely moored, the *St. Roch* rode out the storm.

Reports reached Larsen that this was a bad year for ice, and he almost gave up the idea of completing the voyage during 1944. Indeed, nets had been set to catch fish for the dogs during the winter months, when the ice began to show signs of cracking and the weather improved. Larsen decided to make a dash for Herschel Island. At last, luck was with him and leads appeared in the ice that seemed to have been made for the *St. Roch*. The ship did not stop even when an ice floe carrying seven polar bears passed by. There was no time for hunting if they were to reach the safety of Herschel. Once again, they reached harbour just in time to avoid a storm.

Next morning, to Larsen's surprise, ice conditions were excellent. It seemed that the *St. Roch* would not have to winter in the ice. Taking a risk, Larsen decided to make a bid for home. The Inuit family was quickly put ashore, a hut fixed up for them, ten tons of coal unloaded, and then the ship headed south.

Radio communication with Point Barrow revealed that the ice ahead was fast becoming solid: it promised to be the worst winter in years. Hugging the shore-line and sailing through thick fog, the *St. Roch* rounded the point and passed through the Bering Strait. This meant that the ship had reached the Pacific Ocean and that the long voyage from Halifax would soon end successfully in Vancouver. On October 16, the *St. Roch* docked in Vancouver Harbour. Larsen had brought his ship through 12,000 kilometres of sometimes uncharted waters in only 86 days, becoming the first man ever to sail the Northwest Passage in both directions.

When Larsen's son, Gordon, gained his wings from the R.C.A.F. Larsen was invited to make the presentation himself.

Relics of the North

Chapter 11

As they had made their way westward, finding traces of
earlier, failed expeditions and leaving records of their
own progress, Larsen had developed a great respect for
the old explorers.

> I fancied I could see their tall ships and felt I was on hal-
> lowed ground. I pictured them wintering in isolation and
> discomfort in crowded ships, optimistically waiting for spring
> and better ice conditions. Some of them perished, all risked
> death to carry the proud flag into new territory.

Larsen and his crew found many relics of their voyages,
perfectly preserved by the intense cold.

During the winter of 1941, Larsen made a patrol to
various settlements along the coast of the Boothia
Peninsula. One of his stops was Victoria Harbour, where
the life-style of the Inuit had changed very little since
1829, when Sir John Ross arrived there in his ship
Victory in search of the Northwest Passage. The *Victory*
became locked in the ice, and was abandoned in 1831.

For years, the Inuit regarded her as a treasure chest, a
ready supply of wood and iron for making tools or
weapons. Even one hundred years later, traces of the
ship were still visible. One item in particular, a small
brass cannon turned blue-green with exposure, caught
Larsen's fancy. At 500 kg it was too heavy for his sled, so
he arranged to have it brought back to the *St. Roch* in the
spring.

When spring came, however, the cannon was invisible, buried so deeply in the snow that the Inuit could not
find it, even though the whole settlement turned out
with long poles and probed the snow.

It was ten years before the snow melted sufficiently to
reveal the cannon, and two more years passed before
Larsen was able to see it in its new home, the R.C.M.P.
Museum in Regina. When he had last seen it, age and
exposure had given it a beautiful blueish sheen. Now it
shone like a new coin. One of the duties of the recruits

was to polish it daily. Another century of this, thought Larsen, and the cannon will be polished right out of existence.

Larsen's crew found the remains of other unsuccessful Arctic expeditions — a constant reminder of the dangers they faced themselves. A cenotaph had been erected on Beechey Island in memory of Sir John Franklin and still lying nearby were stocks of coal, shattered barrels, and even the remains of a small yacht, *Mary*, left there in the hope that some survivors of Franklin's crew might find her and sail to safety.

Near Dealey Island, Larsen found a great quantity of ship's stores left behind by Captain Henry Kellett in the expedition of 1853. Unfortunately the bears had broken the containers and scattered the contents all around. Barrels of beef, chocolate, peas and flour lay smashed on the shore. Even rifles had been twisted out of shape. Boats and articles of clothing had been ripped to shreds.

A few tins had survived unbroken so Larsen sent some cans of "Ox Cheek Soup," carrots, and apples to

On lonely Beechey Island this cenotaph is an enduring monument to Sir John Franklin and those who perished while searching for him, and a solemn reminder of the perils faced by all Arctic explorers.

R.C.M.P. headquarters for analysis. Even after so many years it was found that some of the canned food was still edible. Larsen noted the instructions for opening the cans with delight: "Take a hammer and chisel and cut out one end, taking care not to let flakes of paint get into the soup."

Of real value was a beautiful five-metre boat left behind by Captain Joseph Bernier. Two steel runners fastened to the bottom of the boat allowed it to be pulled over the ice very easily. It was far superior to Larsen's boat which was heavy, awkward to haul, and worst of all, it leaked. Since Bernier's boat had lain there untouched for years, Larsen felt that an exchange of boats was quite fair.

Tablets commemorating Arctic explorers who had lost their lives were discovered. The most striking was put up by Lady Franklin to honour her husband.

But the most interesting and most important tablet of all was erected in 1909 by Captain Bernier. It was found near McClure Strait, a large copper plate with the

Born in Quebec in 1852, Joseph Bernier made twelve voyages through the Arctic and explored the region extensively on behalf of the Canadian government. He was largely responsible for asserting Canada's claim to the Arctic Islands. Why is the Canadian Arctic now considered to be an area of "strategic importance?"

Larsen and his crew examine relics of the yacht Mary, *left on Beechey Island by John Ross, and display some of the 90-year-old cans of soup they found there.*

Canadian coat of arms and the Union Jack at the top. Underneath was this inscription.

THIS MEMORIAL IS ERECTED TODAY TO COMMEMORATE TAKING POSSESSION FOR THE DOMINION OF CANADA, OF THE WHOLE ARCTIC ARCHIPELAGO, LYING TO THE NORTH OF AMERICA. FROM LONG. 60W TO 141W UP TO LAT. 90 NORTH. WINTER HRB., MELVILLE ISLAND, C.G.S. "ARCTIC." JULY 1ST 1909, J.E. BERNIER, COMMANDER, J.V. KOENIG SCULPTOR.

On Dominion Day, so many years ago, Canada assumed control of the entire Arctic region right up to the North Pole.

Henry Larsen's patrol in the Arctic was really a continuation and confirmation of Captain Bernier's claim. Over the years the presence of men such as the Mounties and missionaries has preserved this huge area for Canada.

Remnants of Captain Kellett's store.

Recognition Chapter 12

Many honours were bestowed upon Henry Larsen, in
recognition of his contribution to Arctic exploration.
Following his 1944 expedition a bar was added to his
Polar Medal, and he received the first Massey Medal of
the Royal Canadian Geographical Society, of which he
was made a fellow. He was also made an honorary
member of the Royal Geographical Society in Britain
which awarded him the highly-prized Patron's gold
medal for outstanding personal achievement.

   Larsen was now a celebrity, an equal of the famous
explorers he had admired so much as a boy. While

*Governor-General Massey
presents Henry Larsen with the
first Massey Medal, in 1958.*

waiting for the *St. Roch* to be fitted for her return trip through the Arctic, Larsen was invited to meet J. Edgar Hoover in Washington. Stopping off in New York on the way, Larsen met another great Arctic explorer, Vilhjalmur Stefansson.

Larsen, however, was unaffected by his new fame. Commissioned as sub-inspector of the R.C.M.P. in December 1944 and inspector two years later, he continued to command the *St. Roch* during her last two Arctic voyages of 1945-46 and 1947-48. Happily, he was now able to spend more time with his wife and family in Vancouver.

In 1949, having been master of the ship for twenty-one years, he moved to Ottawa to take command of "G" Division of the R.C.M.P., which controls police work in all of northern Canada. In 1953, Larsen was made superintendent.

His sailing career was not over, however, for the *St. Roch* still had one more record to establish. In 1954, Henry Larsen commanded the *St. Roch* on her final voyage from Halifax to Vancouver through the Panama Canal, making her the first ship ever to circumnavigate the North American continent. Shortly afterwards, the *St. Roch* was withdrawn from service, and was purchased by the government for just $5000. The *St. Roch* went on display in the city of Vancouver in 1958.

Superintendent Larsen retired from the R.C.M.P. in 1961, after almost thirty-three years of service, and settled with his family in Vancouver. Following a brief illness, he died in 1964, at the age of 65. He was buried in the R.C.M.P. cemetery in Regina.

Henry Larsen on his retirement from the force in 1961.

Chapter 13 The *St. Roch* Preserved

Many ships have sailed the Arctic seas following Larsen's lead. The Canadian Steamship *Hudson* was a 4,700 ton floating laboratory. Furnished with lounges, air-conditioning, showers, and re-inforced steel hulls, she was a far cry from the *St. Roch*. But the Arctic is not easily conquered. The *CSS Hudson,* as the *St. Roch* before her, blew an engine and had to limp into port.

Still bigger ships challenged the Arctic. The *Manhattan,* a United States tanker of 115,000 tons, was sent north to determine the feasibility of shipping oil by tanker, the first steam-ship to sail the Northwest Passage. Despite her size, the trip was not a complete success. The Canadian icebreaker, *John A. Macdonald* had to free the *Manhattan* from the ice that threatened to entrap her.

At the other end of the scale, the *Skidegate,* a Canadian Coast Guard training vessel only 27 metres long made the difficult west to east crossing of the Arctic.

By boat, by airplane and by snowmobile the mysteries of the Arctic are being solved. In 1958 an American atomic-powered submarine travelled under the ice across the North Pole.

The President of Panarctic Oils Limited of Calgary forsees what he calls the "ultimate ship — 2,000,000 tons and 200 000 horsepower to penetrate the Arctic 12 months of the year."

With all the activity in the Arctic there is no danger that the achievements of the *St. Roch* and her captain will ever be forgotten.

In 1962, the *St. Roch* was proclaimed a National Historic Site, and at once plans were put into effect to repair the damage suffered through time and to restore her as closely as possible to the state in which she had sailed the Northwest Passage.

Parks Canada was assigned the task of refurnishing the vessel. It was decided that the *St. Roch* be restored to

R.C.M.POLICE.S^T.ROCH

The restored St. Roch, *exactly as it was during the 1944 voyage. The Inuit family on board lived in the tent on deck. Notice the long sled stowed on the foredeck.*

the condition she was in for her 1944 trip.

It was a difficult task but eventually, with the assistance of former crew members, the *St. Roch* was restored in the most minute detail, from the buttons on the tunics to the diesel engines. To gain authenticity even the brass pulls on the cupboards were remade to match the originals. Fibre glass was inserted into the hull to stop the dry rot.

The *St. Roch* is now on permanent display in the Vancouver Maritime Museum. The only thing lacking is the yapping of the huskies huddled together for warmth.

Further Reading

Larsen, Henry. *The Big Ship*. McClelland & Stewart Ltd.

Tranter, G. J. *Ploughing the Arctic*. Longmans, Green & Co.

Neatby, L. H. *In Quest of the North West Passage*. Longmans, Green & Co.

The North West Passage. The Queen's Printer, Ottawa.

Larsen, Henry. *The Conquest of the North West Passage*.
Reprinted from the Geographical Journal, Vol. CX, 1947.

Clarke, Tom E. *The Mounties' Patrol of the Sea*. Westminster Press.

R.C.M.P. *The Two Voyages of the St. Roch*. The Queen's Printer.

Thompson, John Beswarick. *The More Northerly Route*. Parks Canada.

Wilkinson, Doug. *Arctic Fever*. Clarke, Irwin & Co. Ltd.

Credits

The author wishes to thank Mrs. Henry Larsen and former crew members J. Olsen and J. Diplock for the information and assistance they generously provided; and Mrs. S. Wilson of St. Catharines Library for her help with research.

The publishers wish to express their gratitude to Mr. Wayne Colwell, of Parks Canada, whose assistance during the preparation of this manuscript was invaluable; to Mr. Gerard Finn also of Parks Canada; to Mrs. H. Larsen and Mr. G. Larsen, for permission to use material belonging to the Larsen family; and to the following who authorized the use of copyright material in this book:

Larsen family collection pages 13, 14, 19, 20, 26, 29, 30, 37, 41, 54, 56, 58, 59

N.F.B., page 11

Parks Canada, page 63

Public Archives of Canada, pages 5 (C-4727, C-9527), 6 (C-17727), 7 (c-1352), 9 (C-9686), 33 (C-21949), 46 (C-70771)

R.C.M.P. Reference, pages 1, 16, 18, 24-5, 34, 43, 44, 49, 50-1, 57, 61 and cover

Index